Miss Grief

PERFORMANCE EDITION

Adapted from "Miss Grief"
by Constance Fenimore Woolson

by Querida Funck

Published by Lemery House Press

Copyright

Dedication

For every woman whose work was dismissed as
"too strange," "too bold," or "too much."
For those who kept writing anyway.

Foreword

This title is part of the *Whispers of Forgotten Women* series—stories in which the lost, the overlooked, and the unheard speak again. Each piece revives a woman's voice history nearly silenced, and pairs it with insights from the stage and recording booth.

In about thirty minutes, *Miss Grief* delivers a complete arc you can program anywhere—classrooms, book clubs, libraries, salons, or small theatres—while still leaving time for Q&A or a companion piece. It's a compact study of recognition and the cost of being heard, ideal for practicing subtle performance and inviting audiences to wrestle with who gets called "genius" (and who doesn't). Intentional Listening Rating: PG–13 for mature themes and emotional intensity.

Constance Fenimore Woolson (1840–1894) wrote of isolation and misunderstanding long before those words became modern concerns. Her heroines live at the margins of art, ambition, and society—struggling to be heard in rooms that were never built for them.

About the Series

True Voice Shorts is a curated collection of enhanced audio and literary performance editions that reimagine classic works, essays, and fables through contemporary voice. Some are adaptations; others are new stories inspired by forgotten lives. Together they create a library of listening—brief in length, lasting in resonance.

The *Whispers of Forgotten Women* theme restores neglected voices from history and literature. These are stories of women who endured in silence, resisted through art, or simply lived fully in times that asked them not to. Each edition pairs the original work with contextual essays and storytelling guides—inviting performers and readers alike to listen between the lines.

About the Authors

Querida Funck is a writer, playwright, voice artist, and stage director whose work explores identity, memory, and voice. As founder of Lemery House Press and creator of the *True Voice Shorts* series, she bridges literary craft and performance practice—bringing the emotional truth of the text forward through tone, rhythm, and restraint.

Constance Fenimore Woolson (1840–1894) was an American author and the grandniece of novelist James Fenimore Cooper. Her own voice, however, was distinct—psychologically rich, quietly ironic, and strikingly modern. After early success in American magazines, she broadened her canvas from American settings to Europe, eventually settling abroad and spending much of her later life in Italy. In Rome, Florence, and Venice—surrounded by artists, expatriates, and shifting social codes she composed some of her most haunting work, including "Miss Grief," first published in *Lippincott's Monthly Magazine* in 1877. Woolson's prose is measured and precise; her empathy for outsiders is unsentimental, and her irony cuts softly but deep.

Woolson's fiction examines the interior lives of women—artists, widows, wanderers—struggling to reconcile talent and circumstance within the limits imposed by gender, class, and money. She returns, again and again, to questions of recognition and erasure: who is seen, who is dismissed, and why. Though later critics often framed her legacy beside friendships with better-known male contemporaries, her work stands on its own for its psychological realism and moral clarity. She died in Venice in 1894, leaving a body of writing whose insight continues to guide scholars, performers, and storytellers—inviting modern readers to consider the costs of silence and the courage it takes to persist.

Guide to Effective Storytelling

Historical & Literary Context

When Woolson wrote *Miss Grief* in 1877, women authors were still considered exceptions in the literary world. Publishers courted their work when it was sentimental or moral—but recoiled from anything challenging, intellectual, or bold. Woolson had already published travel sketches and novels that defied easy categorization.

In *Miss Grief,* she turned her focus inward, exposing the subtle cruelty of a culture that applauds male intellect while quietly sidelining female genius.

The story's frame is deceptively simple: a successful male author in Rome encounters a shabby, middle-aged woman who repeatedly seeks him out, asking him to read her play. His condescension is polite but unyielding—until her death forces him to confront what he refused to see. Woolson's irony is devastating precisely because it is quiet. She never preaches; she simply holds a mirror.

In performance, this subtext becomes palpable. The tension lies not in what is said, but in what remains unspoken.

Story Arc & Character Arc

Exposition: The narrator introduces himself as a young, successful author in Rome—self-assured and self-satisfied.

Rising Action: He receives repeated visits from "Miss Grief," who is persistent, shabby, and strange. Eventually he meets her, dismissing her as eccentric until she recites his own words with piercing understanding.

Climax: She begs him to read her manuscript— a play she believes will prove her worth. When he finally does, he is startled by its power but cannot admit it to her without qualification.

Falling Action: His polite advice and subtle criticism mask envy and fear. Her quiet dignity remains intact; she leaves, resolved.

Resolution: Her death—and the loss of her manuscript—reveal his blindness. What he once saw as madness or presumption was, in truth, genius unrecognized.

The story traces two intersecting arcs: his descent from vanity to remorse, and her ascent from invisibility to posthumous vindication.

Actor / Voice Actor Techniques

Performing *Miss Grief* demands restraint. The narrator's voice should carry charm tinged with arrogance—a man accustomed to admiration. Miss Grief's voice, by contrast, is low and deliberate, bearing weight of years and faith in her art. The performer's task is not to exaggerate their contrast, but to let silence, pacing, and tonal shifts reveal it.

- The **narrator**: urbane, polished, quietly self-absorbed. His tone warms only when speaking of himself. Let small pauses suggest discomfort as his self-image begins to crack.
- **Miss Grief (Crief)**: controlled, dignified, with flashes of intensity. Her calmness in the face of dismissal should draw empathy without pity. **Simpson**: The narrator's manservant; dry, observant, faintly ironic. Provides tonal counterpoint and social mirror for the narrator's arrogance.

Treat the story as chamber theatre: the real drama is internal. Small breaths, gentle accelerations, and emotional stillness become the instruments of meaning.

Effective Staging & Embodied Storytelling

For readers or stage performers, *Miss Grief* benefits from intimacy. A table, a lamp, a single chair evoke the claustrophobia of polite rejection. Two actors can easily carry the piece; even one, alternating posture and tone, can bring it to life.

Lighting can serve as metaphor—warm at first, cooling as self-awareness fades, then soft again in remembrance. Avoid melodrama. Let restraint speak louder than tears.

Audience Engagement

For discussion or classroom settings, *Miss Grief* opens questions still urgent today: What is the cost of genius? Who decides which voices are worth hearing? How does gender shape recognition? Encourage reflection through open-ended prompts:

- How does Woolson use irony to expose privilege?
- In what ways does the narrator reveal himself through what he does *not* understand?
- Why might Miss Grief's art be threatening to him?

For live readings, audiences respond best when the storyteller invites quiet rather than applause—ending not in triumph, but in stillness.

Miss Grief

"A conceited fool" is a not uncommon expression. Now, I know that I am not a fool, but I also know that I am conceited. But, candidly, can it be helped if one happens to be young, well and strong, passably good-looking, with some money that one has inherited and more than one has earned—in all, enough to make life comfortable—and if upon this foundation rests also the pleasant superstructure of a literary success?

Success is deserved, I think - certainly it was not lightly gained. Yet even with this I fully appreciate its rarity. Thus, I find myself very well entertained in life: I have all I wish in the way of society, and a deep, though of course carefully concealed, satisfaction in my own little fame, which fame I foster by a gentle system of non-interference. I know that I am spoken of as "that quiet young fellow who writes those delightful little studies of society, you know;" and I live up to that definition.

A year ago I was in Rome, and enjoying life particularly. I had a large number of my acquaintances there, both American and English, and no day passed without its invitation. Of course I understood it: it is seldom that you find a literary man who is good-tempered, well-dressed, sufficiently provided with money, and obedient to all the rules and requirements of "society."

"When found, make a note of it;" and the note was generally an invitation.

One evening, upon returning to my lodgings, my man Simpson informed me that a person had called in the afternoon, and upon learning that I was absent had left not a card, but her name—"Miss Grief." The title lingered. Miss Grief! "Grief has not so far visited me here," I said to myself, dismissing Simpson and seeking my little balcony for a final smoke, "and she shall not now. I shall take care to be 'not at home' to her if she continues to call." And then I fell to thinking of Isabel Abercrombie, in whose society I had spent that and many evenings: they were golden thoughts.

The next day there was an excursion; it was late when I reached my rooms, and again Simpson informed me that Miss Grief had called.

"Is she coming continuously?" I said, half to myself.

"Yes, sir: she mentioned that she should call again."

"How does she look?"

"Well, sir, a lady, but not so prosperous as she was, I should say," answered Simpson, discreetly.

"Young?"

"No, sir."

"Alone?"

"A maid with her, sir."

But once outside on my little high-up balcony with my cigar, I again forgot Miss Grief and whatever she might represent. Who would not forget in that moonlight, with Isabel Abercrombie's face to remember?

The stranger came for a third time, and I was absent; then she let two days pass, and began again. It grew to be a regular dialogue between Simpson and myself when I came in at night: "Grief to-day?"

"Yes, sir."
"What time?"

"Four, sir."

"Happy the man," I thought, "who can keep her confined to a particular hour!"

But I should not have treated my visitor so cavalierly if I had not felt sure that she was eccentric and unconventional—qualities extremely tiresome in a woman no longer young or attractive. If she were not eccentric she would not have persisted in coming to my door day after day in this silent way, without stating her errand, leaving a note, or presenting her credentials in any shape. I made up my mind that she had something to sell—a bit of carving or some intaglio supposed to be antique. It was known that I had a fancy for such oddities. I said to myself,

"She has read or heard of my 'Old Gold' story, or else 'The Buried God,' and she thinks me an idealizing ignoramus upon whom she can impose. Her sepulchral name is at least not Italian; probably she is a sharp countrywoman of mine, turning, by means of the present esthetic craze, an honest penny when she can."

She had called seven times during a period of two weeks without seeing me, when one day I happened to be at home in the afternoon, owing to pouring rain and a fit of doubt concerning Miss Abercrombie. For I had constructed a careful theory of that young lady's characteristics in my own mind, and she had lived up to it delightfully until the previous evening, when with one word she had blown it to atoms and taken flight, leaving me standing, as it were, on a desolate shore, with nothing but a handful of mistaken inductions wherewith to console myself.

I do not know a more exasperating frame of mind, at least for a constructor of theories. I could not write, and so I took up a French novel (I model myself a little on Balzac). I had been turning over its pages but a few moments when Simpson knocked, and, entering softly, said, with just a shadow of a smile on his well-trained face, "Miss Grief." I briefly consigned Miss Grief to all the Furies, and then, as he still lingered—perhaps not knowing where they resided—I asked where the visitor was.

"Outside, sir—in the hall. I told her I would see if you were at home."

"She must be unpleasantly wet if she had no carriage."

"No carriage, sir: they always come on foot. I think she is a little damp, sir."

"Well, let her in; but I don't want the maid. I may as well see her now, I suppose, and end the affair."

"Yes, sir."

I did not put down my book. My visitor should have hearing, but not much more: she had sacrificed her womanly claims by her persistent attacks upon my door. Presently Simpson ushered her in.

"Miss Grief," he said, and then went out, closing the curtain behind him.

A woman—yes, a lady—but shabby, unattractive, and more than middle-aged.

I rose, bowed slightly, and then dropped into my chair again, still keeping the book in my hand. "Miss Grief?" I said interrogatively as I indicated a seat with my eyebrows.

"Not Grief," she answered—"Crief: my name is Crief."

She sat down, and I saw that she held a small flat box.

"Not carving, then," I thought—"probably old lace, something that belonged to Tullia or Lucrezia Borgia." But as she did not speak I found myself obliged to begin: "You have been here, I think, once or twice before?"

"Seven times; this is the eighth."

A silence.

"I am often out; indeed, I may say that I am never in," I remarked carelessly.

"Yes, you have many friends."

"—Who will perhaps buy old lace," I mentally added. But this time I too remained silent; why should I trouble myself to draw her out? She had sought me; let her advance her idea, whatever it was, now that entrance was gained.

But Miss Grief (I preferred to call her so) did not look as though she could advance anything; her black gown, damp with rain, seemed to retreat fearfully to her thin self, while her thin self-retreated as far as possible from me, from the chair, from everything. Her eyes were cast down; an old-fashioned lace veil with a heavy border shaded her face. She looked at the floor, and I looked at her.

I grew a little impatient, but I made up my mind that I would continue silent and see how long a time she would consider necessary to give due effect to her little pantomime. Comedy? Or was it tragedy? I suppose the full five minutes passed thus in our double silence; and that is a long time when two people are sitting opposite each other alone in a small still room.

At last my visitor, without raising her eyes, said slowly, "You are very happy, are you not, with youth, health, friends, riches, fame?"

It was a singular beginning. Her voice was clear, low, and very sweet as she thus enumerated my advantages one by one in a list. I was attracted by it, but repelled by her words, which seemed to me flattery both dull and bold.

"Thanks," I said, "for your kindness, but I fear it is undeserved. I seldom discuss myself even with my friends."

"I am your friend," replied Miss Grief. Then, after a moment, she added slowly, "I have read every word you have written."

I curled the edges of my book indifferently; I am not a fop, I hope, but—others have said the same.

"What is more, I know much of it by heart," continued my visitor. "Wait: I will show you;" and then, without pause, she began to repeat something of mine word for word, just as I had written it.

On she went, and I—listened. I intended interrupting her after a moment, but I did not, because she was reciting so well, and also because I felt a desire gaining upon me to see what she would make of a certain conversation which I knew was coming—a conversation between two of my characters which was, to say the least, sphinxlike, and somewhat incandescent as well.

What won me a little, too, was the fact that the scene she was reciting (it was hardly more than that, though called a story) was secretly my favorite among all the sketches from my pen which a gracious public has received with favor. I never said so, but it was. And I had always felt a wondering annoyance that the aforesaid public, while kindly praising beyond their worth other attempts of mine, had never noticed the higher purpose of this little shaft, aimed not at the balconies and lighted windows of society, but straight up toward the distant stars.

So she went on, and presently reached the conversation: my two people began to talk. She had raised her eyes now, and was looking at me soberly as she gave the words of the woman, quiet, gentle, cold, and the replies of the man, bitter, hot, and scathing.

Her very voice changed, and took, though always sweetly, the different tones required. While no point of meaning, however small, no breath of delicate emphasis which I had meant, but which the dull types could not give, escaped an appreciative and full, almost overfull recognition which startled me. For she had understood me almost better than I understood myself. It seemed to me that while I had labored to interpret a psychological riddle, she, coming after, had comprehended its bearings better than I had, though confining herself strictly to my own words and emphasis.

The scene ended (and it ended rather suddenly), she dropped her eyes, and moved her hand nervously to and for over the box she held; her gloves were old and shabby, her hands small.

I was secretly much surprised by what I had heard, but my ill humor was deep-seated that day, and I still felt sure, that the box contained something which I was expected to buy.

"You recite remarkably well," I said carelessly, "and I am much flattered also by your appreciation of my attempt. But it is not, I presume, to that alone that I owe the pleasure of this visit?"

"Yes," she answered, still looking down, "it is, for if you had not written that scene I should not have sought you. Your other sketches are interiors, exquisitely painted and delicately finished, but of small scope. This is a sketch in a few bold, masterly lines—work of entirely different spirit and purpose."

I was nettled by her insight. "You have bestowed so much of your kind attention upon me that I feel your debtor," I said, conventionally. "It may be that there is something I can do for you—connected, possibly, with that little box?"

It was impertinent, but it was true; for she answered, "Yes."

I smiled, but her eyes were cast down and she did not see the smile.
"What I have to show you is a manuscript," she said after a pause which I did not break; "it is a drama. I thought that perhaps you would read it."

(An authoress! This is worse than old lace,) I said to myself in dismay.—Then, aloud, "My opinion would be worth nothing, Miss Crief."

"Not in a business way, I know. But it might be—an assistance personally." Her voice had sunk to a whisper; outside, the rain was pouring steadily down. She was a very depressing object to me as she sat there with her box.

"I hardly think I have the time at present—" I began.

She had raised her eyes and was looking at me; then, when I paused, she rose and came suddenly toward my chair. "Yes, you will read it," she said with her hand on my arm—"you will read it. Look at this room; look at yourself; look at all you have. Then look at me, and have pity."

I had risen, for she held my arm, and her damp skirt was brushing my knees.

Her large dark eyes looked intently at mine as she went on; "I have no shame in asking. Why should I have? It is my last endeavor; but a calm and well-considered one. If you refuse I shall go away, knowing that Fate has willed it so. And I shall be content."

(She is mad,) I thought. But she did not look so, and she had spoken quietly, even gently.—"Sit down," I said, moving away from her. I felt as if I had been magnetized;

but it was only the nearness of her eyes to mine, and their intensity. I drew forward a chair, but she remained standing.

"I cannot," she said in the same sweet, gentle tone, "unless you promise."

"Very well, I promise; only sit down."

As I took her arm to lead her to the chair I perceived that she was trembling, but her face continued unmoved.

"You do not, of course, wish me to look at your manuscript now?"

I said, temporizing; "it would be much better to leave it. Give me your address, and I will return it to you with my written opinion; though, I repeat, the latter will be of no use to you. It is the opinion of an editor or publisher that you want."

"It shall be as you please. And I will go in a moment," said Miss Grief, pressing her palms together, as if trying to control the tremor that had seized her slight frame.

She looked so pallid that I thought of offering her a glass of wine; then I remembered that if I did it might be a bait to bring her there again, and this I was desirous to prevent. She rose while the thought was passing through my mind. Her pasteboard box lay on the chair she had first occupied; she took it, wrote an address on the cover, laid it down, and then, bowing with a little air of formality, drew her black shawl round her shoulders and turned toward the door.

I followed, after touching the bell. "You will hear from me by letter," I said.

Simpson opened the door, and I caught a glimpse of the maid, who was waiting in the anteroom. She was an old woman, shorter than her mistress, equally thin, and dressed like her in rusty black. As the door opened she turned toward it a pair of small, dim blue eyes with a look of furtive suspense. Simpson dropped the curtain, shutting me into the inner room; he had no intention of allowing me to accompany my visitor further.

But I had the curiosity to go to a bay-window in an angle from whence I could command the street-door, and presently I saw them issue forth in the rain and walk away side by side, the mistress, being the taller, holding the umbrella: probably there was not much difference in rank between persons so poor and forlorn as these.

It grew dark. I was invited out for the evening, and I knew that if I should go I should meet Miss Abercrombie. I said to myself that I would not go. I got out my paper for writing, I made my preparations for a quiet evening at home with myself; but it was of no use. It all ended slavishly in my going. At the last allowable moment I presented myself, and—as a punishment for my vacillation, I suppose—I never spent a more disagreeable evening.

I drove homeward in a murky temper; it was foggy without, and very foggy within. What Isabel really was, now that she had broken through my elaborately built theories, I was not able to decide. There was, to tell the truth, a certain young Englishman—But that is apart from this story.

I reached home, went up to my room, and had supper. It was to console myself; I am obliged to console myself scientifically once in a while. I was walking up and down afterward, smoking and feeling somewhat better, when my eye fell on the pasteboard box. I took it up; on the cover was written an address which showed that my visitor must have walked a long distance in order to see me: "A. Crief."—

"A Grief," I thought; "and so she is. I positively believe she has brought all this trouble upon me: she has the evil eye." I took out the manuscript and looked at it. It was in the form of a little volume, and clearly written; on the cover was the word "Armor" in German text, and, underneath, a pen-and-ink sketch of a helmet, breastplate, and shield.

"Grief certainly needs armor," I said to myself, sitting down by the table and turning over the pages. "I may as well look over the thing now; I could not be in a worse mood." And then I began to read.

Early the next morning Simpson took a note from me to the given address, returning with the following reply: "No; I prefer to come to you; at four; A. Crief." These words, with their three semicolons, were written in pencil upon a piece of coarse printing-paper, but the handwriting was as clear and delicate as that of the manuscript in ink.

"What sort of a place was it, Simpson?"

"Very poor, sir, but I did not go all the way up. The elder person came down, sir, took the note, and asked me to wait where I was."

"You had no chance, then, to make inquiries?" I said, knowing full well that he had emptied the entire neighborhood of any information it might possess concerning these two lodgers.

"Well, sir, you know how these foreigners will talk, whether one wants to hear or not. But it seems that these two people have been there but a few weeks; they live alone, and are uncommonly silent and reserved. The people round there call them something that signifies 'the Madams American, thin and dumb.'"

At four the "Madams American" arrived; it was raining again, and they came on foot under their old umbrella. The maid waited in the anteroom, and Miss Grief ushered into my bachelor's parlor. I had thought that I should meet her with great deference; but she looked so forlorn

14

that my deference changed to pity. It was the woman that impressed me then, more than the writer—the fragile, nerveless body more than the inspired mind. For it was inspired. I had sat up half the night over her drama, and had felt thrilled through and through more than once by its earnestness, passion, and power.

No one could have been more surprised than I was to find myself thus enthusiastic. I thought I had outgrown that sort of thing. And one would have supposed, too (I myself should have supposed so the day before), that the faults of the drama, which were many and prominent, would have chilled any liking I might have felt, I being a writer myself, and therefore critical; for writers are as apt to make much of the "how," rather than the "what," as painters, who, it is well known, prefer an exquisitely rendered representation of a commonplace theme to an imperfectly executed picture of even the most striking subject.

But in this case, on the contrary, the scattered rays of splendor in Miss Grief's drama had made me forget the dark spots, which were numerous and disfiguring; or, rather, the splendor had made me anxious to have the spots removed. And this also was a philanthropic state very unusual with me. Regarding unsuccessful writers, my motto had been "Væ victis!"

My visitor took a seat and folded her hands; I could see, in spite of her quiet manner, that she was in breathless suspense. It seemed so pitiful that she should be trembling there before me—a woman so much older than

I was, a woman who possessed the divine spark of genius, which I was by no means sure (in spite of my success) had been granted to me—that I felt as if I ought to go down on my knees before her, and entreat her to take her proper place of supremacy at once.

But there! one does fall to one's knees before a woman over fifty, plain in feature, thin, dejected, and ill-dressed. I contented myself with taking her hands (in their miserable old gloves) in mine, while I said cordially, "Miss Crief, your drama seems to me full of original power. It has roused my enthusiasm: I sat up half the night reading it."

The hands I held shook, but something made me tighten my hold and bestow upon her a reassuring smile. She looked at me for a moment, and then, suddenly and noiselessly, tears rose and rolled down her cheeks. I dropped her hands and retreated. I had not thought her tearful: on the contrary, her voice and face had seemed rigidly controlled.

But now here she was bending herself over the side of the chair with her head resting on her arms, not sobbing aloud, but her whole frame shaken by the strength of her emotion. I rushed for a glass of wine and pressed her to take it. I did not quite know what to do, but, putting myself in her place, I decided to praise the drama; and praise it I did. I do not know when I have used so many adjectives. She raised her head and began to wipe her eyes.

"Do take the wine," I said, interrupting myself in my torrent or overwhelming flow of words.

"I dare not," she answered, then added humbly, "that is, unless you have a biscuit here or a bit of bread."

I found some biscuits; she ate two, and then slowly drank the wine, while I resumed my verbal Niagara. Under its influence—and that of the wine too, perhaps—she began to show new life. It was not that she looked radiant, but simply that she looked warm. I now perceived what had been the principal discomfort of her appearance heretofore: it was that she had looked all the time as if suffering from cold.

At last I could think of nothing more to say, and stopped. I really admired the drama, but I thought I had exerted myself sufficiently as an anti-hysteric, and that adjectives enough, for the present at least, had been administered She had put down her empty wineglass, and was resting her hands on the broad cushioned arms of her chair with, for a thin person, a sort of expanded content.

"You must pardon my tears," she said, smiling; "it was the revulsion of feeling. My life was at a low ebb: if your sentence had been against me it would have been my end."

"Your end?"

"Yes, the end of my life; I should have destroyed myself."

"Then you would have been a weak as well as wicked woman," I said in a tone of disgust. I do hate sensationalism.

"Oh no, you know nothing about it. I should have destroyed only this poor worn tenement of clay. But I can well understand how you would look upon it. Regarding the desirableness of life the prince and the beggar may have different opinions.—We will say no more of it, but talk of the drama instead."

As she spoke the word "drama" a triumphant brightness came into her eyes.

I took the manuscript from a drawer and sat down beside her. "I suppose you know that there are faults," I said, expecting ready acquiescence.

"I was not aware that there were any," was her gentle reply.

Here was a beginning! After all my interest in her—and, I may say under the circumstances, my kindness — she received me in this way! However, my belief in her genius was too sincere to be altered by her whimsies; so I persevered. "Let us go over it together," I said. "Shall I read it to you, or will you read it to me?"

"I will not read it, but recite it."

"That will never do; you will recite it so well that we shall see only the good points, and what we have to concern ourselves with now is the bad ones."

"I will recite it," she repeated.

"Now, Miss Crief," I said bluntly, "for what purpose did you come to me? Certainly not merely to recite. I am no stage manager. Is it not the idea that I might help you in obtaining a publisher?"

"Yes, yes," she answered, looking at me apprehensively, all her old manner returning.

I followed up my advantage, opened the little paper volume and began. I first took the drama line by line, and spoke of the faults of expression and structure; then I turned back and touched upon two or three glaring impossibilities in the plot. "Your absorbed interest in the motive of the whole no doubt made you forget these blemishes," I said apologetically.

But, to my surprise, I found that she did not see the blemishes—that she appreciated nothing I had said, comprehended nothing. Such unaccountable obtuseness puzzled me. I began again, going over the whole with even greater minuteness and care. I worked hard: the perspiration stood in beads upon my forehead as I struggled with her—what shall I call it—obstinacy? But it was not exactly obstinacy. She simply could not see the faults of her own work no more than a blind man can see the smoke that dims a patch of blue sky.

When I had finished my task the second time she still remained as gently impassive as before. I leaned back in my chair exhausted, and looked at her.

A few days later, word comes that she has died—alone, her manuscript left behind like a final act of faith.

The narrator learns it too late. He searches for her, perhaps out of guilt, perhaps out of something he cannot quite name—but finds only an empty room and the faint trace of her presence.
Her *Armor* was more than a title. It was her defense—the fragile shield of conviction she carried against a world that would not see her.

And so she endures, not through fame or recognition, but through the truth she refuses to surrender.

To speak her name now is to honor every unseen voice— every story dismissed before it had the chance to live.

Miss Grief reminds us that brilliance does not always blaze in its own time. Sometimes, it waits—quietly—for someone willing to listen.

Wrap-Up: Storytelling in Context

Miss Grief bridges literature and performance through silence. The narrator's blindness becomes the audience's awakening: we recognize genius only after it has fallen quiet. In reading or performance, the story reminds us that empathy often arrives too late—but still matters. Each retelling reclaims that empathy sooner, asking us to notice whose work is dismissed and how easily "polite" critique can eclipse courage.

For performers, the lesson lies in restraint. Woolson's prose thrives on understatement and negative space; the most truthful beats happen between the lines. Let the audience do part of the work—arrive late to emotions, release them slowly, and resist explaining what the text has already earned. The actor's responsibility is to hold tension with honesty, to let stillness hurt without pushing it toward melodrama. Think in breath lengths: shorter on the narrator's vanity, longer on Miss Grief's steadiness; a full beat of quiet after moments of recognition.

Practical tips for common settings (easy to implement):

Classroom / Book Club

- Open with a 30-second frame: who Woolson was and the question "Who gets to be recognized as 'genius'?"

- Read in two voices (Narrator / Miss Grief) seated at the front; music is unnecessary—let silence be the underscore.
- Mark three planned pauses for discussion: after the first encounter, after the recitation, after the manuscript scene.
- Give two exit questions: "Where did empathy fail?" and "What would 'seeing her in time' have required?"

Library Salon / Live Storytelling Night

- Keep the footprint simple: two chairs and a small table with a lamp; dim to warm light at start, fade slightly cooler during critique passages, and warm again for the final reflection.
- Face slightly off-axis rather than straight out; it reads as more intimate.
- Pace guide: begin brisk (narrator's charm), settle into measured tempo for Miss Grief, and allow one full breath of silence after her "last endeavor" line.
- Leave two minutes for audience reflection before Q&A; do not rush the final quiet.

Small Stage / Readers' Theatre

- Music bed is optional; if used, keep pre/post only (no underbed during text). A single bell or cue light can mark scene turns.
- Stand–sit contrast: narrator standing for confidence, Miss Grief seated for economy, then reverse positions after the manuscript to signal the power shift.
- Prop discipline: one manuscript, one shawl; nothing else.

22

- Mic technique: stay close and steady; let dynamics come from phrasing, not volume spikes.

Across settings, aim for clarity over adornment: clean sightlines, unhurried breaths, and intentional pauses where the audience must fill the silence. That's where *Miss Grief* does its deepest work.

Epilogue & Bonus Reading

Woolson and the Price of Being Heard

Constance Fenimore Woolson wrote from the margins of both gender and geography. In *Miss Grief*, she captured the loneliness of the woman artist—the ache of knowing one's worth in a world determined to overlook it. Her quiet rebellion still resonates. She refused to make her art small enough to fit the expectations around her.

Woolson's own life mirrored the themes she wrote. Born into a respected American family, she published travel sketches and fiction that earned praise but little security. Like her character in *Miss Grief*, she lived much of her later life abroad, often alone, navigating the contradictions of independence and isolation.

In Rome and later Venice, she moved among expatriate artists, including Henry James. Their friendship—sometimes mentorship, sometimes rivalry—echoes through this story's undercurrents: the confident male observer, the woman artist defined by his gaze.

After Woolson's death, James would serve as her literary executor, editing her legacy with both admiration and unease.

Miss Grief anticipates modern feminist criticism by decades. It exposes the polite mechanisms that erase women's art—not through censorship or scandal, but through the subtle condescension of praise laced with disbelief.

That dynamic endures. The story remains a quiet protest against dismissal disguised as civility, and a testament to the resilience of artists who refuse to disappear.

To tell her story today is to honor every artist who has waited for the door to open.

CR

A modernized adaptation of "Jeannette" from *Castle Nowhere: Lake-Country Sketches* (1875) by Constance Fenimore Woolson modernized for use as a monologue (~3.5-5 minutes)

Jeannette

(Warmly, with gentle nostalgia.)
Up in the straits where Lake Huron meets Lake Michigan, there's an island that remembers you if you've ever loved it.

We called it Mackinac — a half-moon harbor, white fort, cedar air so clean it rang in your lungs.

I spent a winter there, when the ice locked us in and the world below felt like another century.

(A fond laugh.)
That's where I met Jeannette — petite Jeanneton — the fisherman's daughter.
French, English, a touch of Ojibwe, and somehow all grace.

Her eyes were blue, her hair black, her laughter bright as the gulls.
She came to teach me beadwork — and, heaven help me, patience.
Our surgeon would pass through — Rodney Prescott, silent as a sermon.

Jeannette fluttered for his notice; he barely saw her.

"No mind in that face," he said once. He was wrong.

Her mind was music — only no one had ever taught her the notes.

(Pause. Tenderly.)
So I did. A B C. Ivry by Macaulay. "Charge for the golden lilies…" she'd cry, her accent turning war into song.

And I thought — if the world could hear her voice just once without judgment, they might understand what beauty really is.
(Softly.)
But the world rarely listens to such voices for long.
Some brilliance is too delicate for parade-ground drills.

(Beat — closing.)
I still see her sometimes, in dreams of that island — hair loose, beads catching the firelight.

We teach what we can, when we can.
The rest … we carry in memory.

Director's Script Appendix

Narrator's Accent & Voice Guide

Vocal Character

The narrator's voice should feel **cultivated yet contemporary** — articulate, musical, and intimate. Think of a modern storyteller bringing 19th-century prose to life, not an imitation of Victorian speech.

Accent Foundation

- **Primary Base:** Neutral American (General American / light Mid-Atlantic blend).
  - *r* is gently voiced, never harsh.
  - Vowels open and forward — *thought* → /thawt/, not /thaw-ut/.
- **Regional Warmth:** A trace of upper-Midwestern color is welcome — soften "a" and "o" for realism — but keep clarity for wide audiences.
- **Historical Flavor:** A light British cadence may appear in formal or reflective lines; use it as rhythm, not imitation.

Tone & Placement

- Forward, resonant mask rather than chest voice.
- Crisp consonants ("t," "d," "g") for intelligibility.
- Shape long sentences with fluid melodic arcs; breathe at commas, not periods.

Emotional Register

- **Opening:** Conversational, curious, touched with irony.

- **Middle:** Warm, compassionate — accent softens as empathy deepens.
- **Closing:** Centered, gentle resonance; linger slightly on sustained vowels in key phrases.

Avoid

Over-clipped British RP, nasal Midwestern, or theatrical "period" affectations. The storyteller bridges centuries, not impersonates them.

Performance Notes

Tempo & Pacing: Approx. 130–140 words per minute. Honor Woolson's rhythm — let pauses breathe but never stall momentum. Use half-beats between shifts in tone or emotional image.

Physical Presence
- Opening: Open stance, lifted focus, as if addressing a horizon.
- Middle: Seated or relaxed posture for intimacy.
- Quoting Other Characters: Quarter-turn or change of eyeline to indicate perspective shift.
- Closing: Stillness — centered, facing front, small release of breath on final line.

Vocal Texture & Dynamics
- Begin with brightness and air.
- Add warmth through middle range on descriptive lines.
- Reserve low, rounded tones for introspection or loss.
- Let soft consonants shape emotional detail ("ce," "th," "f").

Character Accent Notes

- **Simpson:** Subtle English servant inflection — dry, precise, lightly ironic.
- **Miss Crief:** Educated American with traces of weariness; clear diction, slightly slowed pace.
- **The Narrator**: Confident mid-Atlantic narrator tone evolving toward humility.

Best Use for Auditions or Showcases

Ideal for roles emphasizing reflective intelligence, emotional restraint, and historical realism.
Strong audition choice for:

- *Our Town* (Emily or Stage Manager)
- *The Glass Menagerie* (Laura or Amanda)
- *Little Women* (Marmee)
- *Silent Sky* (Henrietta Leavitt)
- *Arcadia* (Hannah Jarvis)
  Also effective for narration reels, historical radio pieces, and literary voiceover samples.

More from Lemery House Press

Discover more stories of reflection, resilience, and
imagination in the *True Voice Shorts* series.
Available in enhanced audio and literary editions at:
www.LemeryHousePress.com

Listen. Read. Remember.

www.ingramcontent.com/pod-product-compliance
Lightning Source LLC
Chambersburg PA
CBHW051336120626
46547CB00016B/2570